AFRICAN LEGACY
UPLIFTED

ANCIENT EGYPT

VOLUME ONE

ISBN: 978-1-7362654-1-3

www.bernardmcarthur.com

African Legacy Uplifted: Ancient Egypt

First Edition

Cover and interior designed by David Ter-Avanesyan/Ter33Design

Egypt map by PaPicasso/Shutterstock.com

AFRICAN LEGACY
UPLIFTED

ANCIENT EGYPT

VOLUME ONE

BERNARD McARTHUR

CONTENTS

Egypt

Before launching my travel agency, I retired from twenty-five years of service as a Special Agent/ Law Enforcement officer with the U.S. Federal Government Office of Labor Racketeering in New York. I was promoted to Special Agent in Philadelphia and Atlanta Regions. I have since traveled the world and shared the experience with thousands of people.

Back in 2012 I went to Egypt with my travel company, Dancin' Doug Travel (DDT). With my background in law enforcement, we at DDT put an emphasis on fun, fellowship, and a safe and secure travel experience. On my first excursion to Egypt, I took 110 people in three groups, which required me to stay there for a month. This time gave me additional insight into the true history of Egypt.

We traveled throughout Egypt and visited Cairo, Memphis, the Saqqara, Aswan, the Island of Philae, the Temple of Horus, the Valley of the Kings, the Nubian Village, Kum Ombo, and Luxor.

In 2019 DDT returned to Egypt with another large group of 106 people. This time we added Alexandria to the itinerary in addition to touring the great Museum of Cairo. A high point of the trip was the expressions on faces when we provided school supplies from our fundraiser for children of the Nubian Village.

Those travelers can go back and tell their children to take pride in excelling in math or science. They will tell their children, "Your ancestors built the first Wonder of the World—a mathematical phenomenon that still has not been fully understood or completely analyzed to this day.". I relished seeing that pivotal moment when Black people recognized how their history had been purposely misrepresented, especially by Hollywood and in academic textbooks, almost all of which show the Egyptians as anything but Black people.

I am glad Bernard McArthur traveled to Egypt, Africa, with me. We have been friends a long time, and he is one of the most dedicated people I know. He always wants to elevate those around him. I know you will enjoy the pictures he took as he shares with you what he saw from his unique perspective.

Douglas Colon, CEO
DDT Contracting Services, INC

The history of Egypt transcends more than thirty dynasties, each of which has contributed significant intellectual and architectural advancements to civilization. Although Egypt has a rich cultural heritage, before the first major invasion occurring in 1675 B.C.E., indigenous Africans ruled the nation.

During the eighteenth dynasty the Hyksos people of Persian decent invaded Egypt and ruled Egypt for approximately two hundred years. The Hyksos were eventually expelled from Egypt by Ahmose I and the indigenous people of Africa once again gained control of Egypt for a thousand years. The Egyptian rulers once again lost control around 616 B.C.E. and were invaded by the Persians, Greeks, Romans, and the Arab nation. Additionally, there was a period where Egypt was under French and British control.

Egypt was known as Kemet, until about 600 B.C.E. Currently, Egypt is known as the Arab Republic of Egypt.

Many societies have been enamored by ancient Egypt's civilization and culture. Ancient Egypt has a rich cultural history reflecting a keen knowledge of science, a complex and hierarchical governmental structure, and monumental edifices that have withstood weather conditions, invasions, and destruction. Egypt's culture was so advanced in that Egyptians had the skill and knowledge to undertake intricate medical procedures and surgeries and perfected the mummification process. Prevalent throughout Egyptian culture was the architectural skill which led to the construction of pyramids, monuments, and temples. Ancient Egypt has one of the oldest known African civilizations and scholars all over the world have been astonished after discovering what life was like before attacks from neighboring countries.

Throughout the ages, ancient Egypt's true history became muddled as outside invaders plundered its libraries and claimed its ingenuity and intellectual advancements. There were instances where historical books and scrolls were burned, and Egypt's history was absorbed by other cultures.

The true history of Egypt can never be erased as it is documented on the walls of tombs, imprinted on papyrus scrolls and etched along various monumental structures.

After the major invasion of Alexander, the Great, ancient Egypt's history was transformed and much of its history was claimed by various ruling empires. For thousands of years African heritage was distorted, and accomplishments were erroneously attributed to other cultures.

Many of Egypt's treasures have been pillaged and after numerous invasions, countless artifacts have been stolen and taken to other countries. As a result of the plundering, several of Egypt's precious relics are on display throughout the world. Fortunately, with technological advances many hidden gems have been uncovered and once again present the true history of Egypt.

I have sought to photograph and visually present images of what is often the unknown history of the African nation of Egypt. Like many before me, I have studied the history of this intriguing culture, however my photojournalism is unique as it captures and documents the extraordinary Egyptian culture. I gained a wealth of insight traveling throughout the country with three renowned Egyptologists as well as studying under the late Dr. Josef A. A. Ben-Jochannan a world-renowned and highly respected professor who spent his life researching Egyptian history.

In the book we explore various aspects of ancient Egyptian culture—the Great Pyramids, the pharaohs, and the ruling kings and queens of ancient Egypt.

There is a great deal of world history that comes out of Africa, from the oldest human fossil dating back millions of years ago to the development of the 365-day calendar. One book cannot capture and uncover the full history and contributions of Africa. I want to encourage the reader to research Egypt's many discoveries and accomplishments and I invite the reader to take in the photographs and observe the rich historical innovation stemming from African culture. I want this book to inspire youth and encourage children to learn more about the positive aspects of African history that extend far beyond slavery. Africa's rich inclusive history should be included in textbooks and studied by students.

Some of the photographs in the book feature images of artifacts and monuments that date back more than four thousand years. The Egyptians were known to document their stories on tombs and on gigantic edifices using paintings, carvings, papyrus, and hieroglyphics. I implore the reader to take in the monuments in existence for thousands of years.

Egyptians practiced a myriad of religions, worshiped several deities, and engaged in various forms of religious rituals. Royal family members were taught Egyptian philosophy and trained in the Egyptian school of thought. Aristotle, the Greek philosopher studied in Egypt for many years and scholars and philosophers from all over the world came to Egypt during their quests for knowledge.

Herodotus, a Greek historian from 450 B.C.E. described the people of ancient Egypt as having thick lips, wooly hair, and burnt skin and when viewing the images of ancient Egypt, you will notice the pronounced indigenous African facial features prevalent in paintings, temples, monuments, and relics. Without a doubt, the pronounced attributes of Africans are unmistakably prevalent throughout these artifacts.

Looking at the structure of temples and pyramids, it is easy to comprehend the complex mathematical and scientific genius used to build these edifices and appreciate the advanced knowledge of the Egyptians. For example, in order to construct the massive structures of the pyramids, Egyptians had to transport millions of massive stone blocks weighing approximately 2.5 tons without any of the construction and machinery tools available today. Many of these structures have been able to withstand the elements for thousands of years and are still intact.

In Egypt the pharaohs, kings, queens, and high priests, were the most important figures to rule the country. As depicted in the movie *Black Panther*, the king, queen, and royal families are often seen with crossed arms over their chest in many Egyptian relics. Additionally, in many Egyptian artifacts and historical sites, royalty is depicted holding a crook and flail with arms crossed denoting kingship and royalty. There were periods in Egypt when women ruled Egypt, either with a king or as a king/queen pharaoh.

In many images women were shown with braided hair, an art form practiced throughout the world today. In one instance, a female pharaoh named Hatshepsut once ruled Egypt as a great pharaoh and queen. She was able to move throughout the palace and society as a pharaoh, at times disguising herself as a man, and ruled Egypt as long as most of the male pharaohs. She was a fierce warrior and led her army to battle while also distinguishing herself as a visionary master builder and her influence is prevalent throughout Karnak, Egypt.

The obelisk in Washington, D.C, is similar to Cleopatra's Needle located in Central Park in New York City and it and it evokes a feeling of euphoria to know that our ancestors constructed it over a thousand years ago. Cleopatra's needle was erected in Egypt over three thousand years ago and transported from Egypt to New York City.

In Karnak, Egypt obelisks of Pharaoh Hatshepsut and her father, Thutmose I still stand thousands of years later.

There were many great pharaohs, both male and female, who made significant cultural contributions to Egypt, however, much of their history has been removed from Egyptian temples. It was said that some rulers even tried to remove the history of Pharaoh Hatshepsut from historical records. Additionally, during some invasions libraries were plundered, and historical records were destroyed by fire.

The notable Pharaoh Ramesses II ruled Egypt for more than sixty years and Pharaohs Khufu, Khafre, and Menkaure were said to be responsible for building the Great Pyramids of Giza. It is said that the Great Sphinx of Giza has the face of Pharaoh Khafre. Another queen, Nefertiti, was known to be a wise ruler of Egypt revered for her beauty and intellect. During her lifetime, Queen Nefertiti was treated as an equal to her husband, Pharaoh Akhenaten.

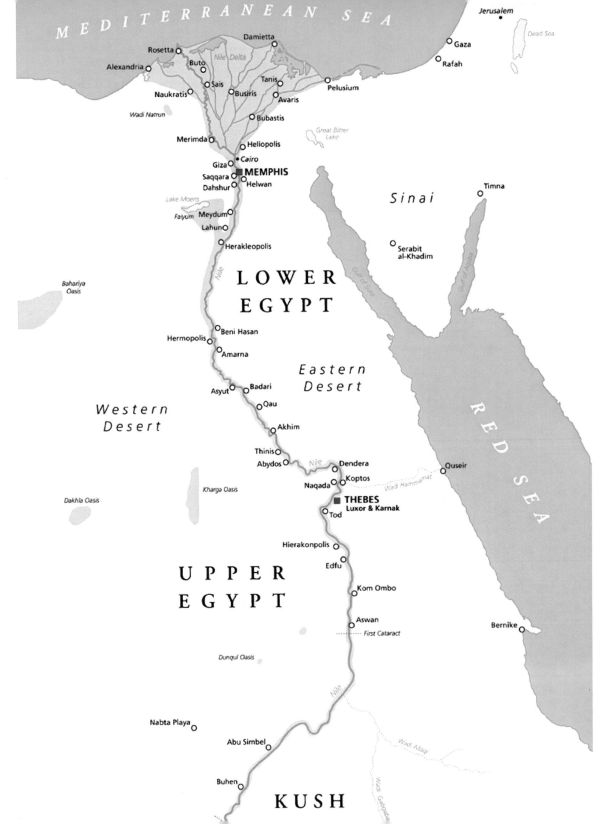

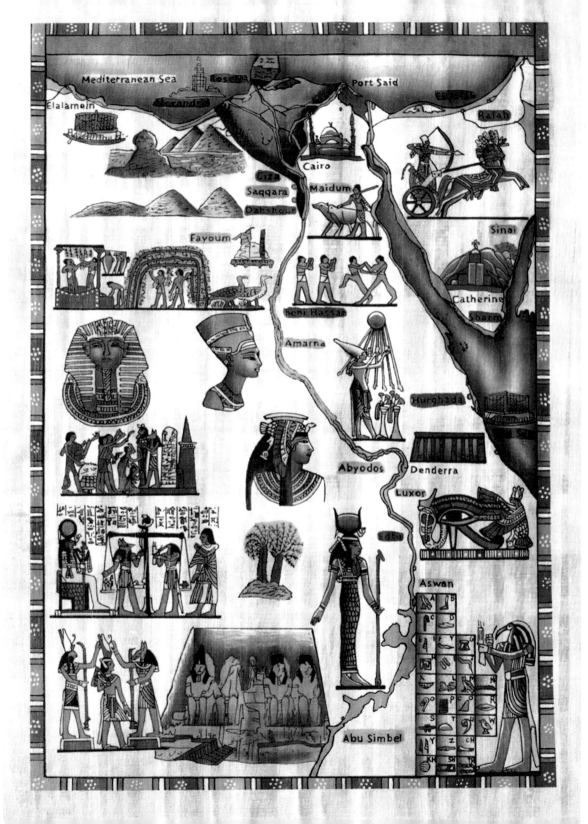

GIZA

The pyramids of Khufu, Khafre, and the Menkaure are located in Giza and have withstood the elements of time. The Great Sphinx is also located in Giza and it is said that the sphinx was built for Pharaoh Khafre. The sphinx has the face of King Khafre and the body of a lion and it is believed that the sphinx is guarding the tomb of Khafre and warding off evil spirits.

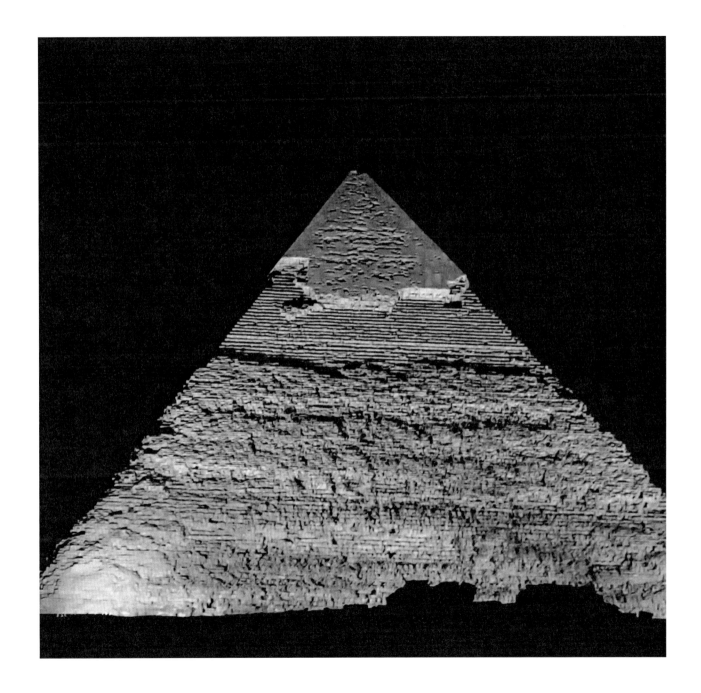

LIFE ON THE NILE RIVER

The Nile River extends for more than four thousand miles and there a great number of historical sites that surround it. The Nile River played an important role to Egypt as it served as ancient Egypt's water supply, major route of travel, and important trade route. Additionally, many temples were constructed along its banks. Each year the river overflows and deposits rich topsoil on its banks contributing to plentiful harvests. As experts in agricultural planning, the Egyptians learned to manage the river cycles and developed a 365-day lunar calendar which helped to successfully sustain the land during the entire year.

MORTUARY TEMPLE OF HATSHEPSUT

The Mortuary Temple of Hatshepsut is located beneath the cliff of Deir el-Bahari. Pharaoh Hatshepsut was a female pharaoh, and her influence can be seen throughout Egypt. She ruled as both king and queen and was one of the longest-ruling pharaohs in Egypt, ruling for more than twenty years. Pharaoh Hatshepsut was a prolific master builder and warrior and she extended peace and trade throughout Egypt. She constructed amazing obelisks that can be seen at the Karnak Temple site however, after her death, her name was overwritten on some of the structures as individuals attempted to erase her name from history.

COLOSSI OF MEMNON

Colossi of Memnon are two monumental statues of Pharaoh Amenhotep III who ruled around 1390 B.C.E. and these statues are said to be guardians of his mortuary temple. Over the years the complex was eroded due to hurricanes, floods, and earthquakes however these statues are the few remaining structures of a larger funerary complex.

KARNAK TEMPLE

Along the Nile River, the Karnak Temple was dedicated to deities and is the largest temple complex in the world. For more than 1,300 years, thirty pharaohs contributed to the temple and construction ended during the Roman invasion of Egypt.

THE VALLEY OF THE KINGS

The tombs of many pharaohs lie in the valley surrounded by mountains located on the west bank of the Nile River in the Theban Hills. Over the last one hundred years, historians excavated over sixty-two tombs, discovering buried kings, queens, and other royalty. Interestingly, each tomb was carved into the mountain.

Although many of the tombs were robbed, the walls of the tombs were decorated with intricate themes including the passage through the underworld. Some scenes depict the lives of royalty traveling through the underworld after death.

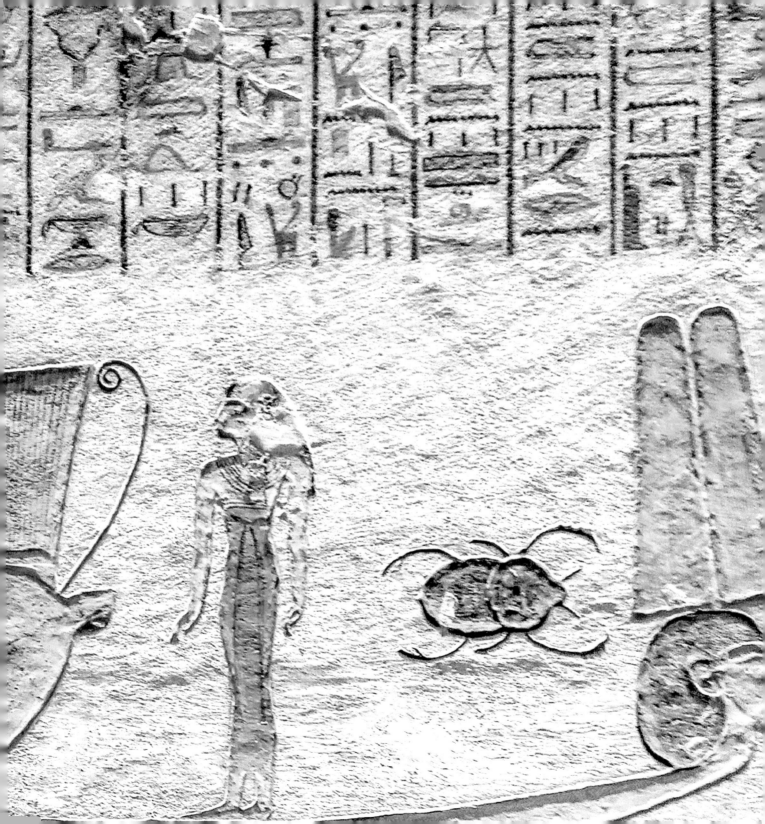

KING TUTANKHAMUN'S TOMB

King Tutankhamun was known to be the youngest ruler of ancient Egypt. He was the son of Pharaoh Akhenaten and Queen Nefertiti and was 8 or 9 years old when he became Pharaoh. During his reign, he initiated many building projects visible at the temple of Karnak. Unfortunately, King Tutankhamun died suddenly at the age of nineteen. In 1922 archaeologists Harvard Carver unearthed King Tutankhamun's tomb and many of the contents of the tomb were intact. Many of King Tutankhamun's treasurers are on display at the Cairo Museum in Egypt.

THE TEMPLE OF HORUS AT EDFU

The temple is located on the west bank of the Nile River and is dedicated to Horus the son of Isis and Osiris. Construction of the structure took place during the Ptolemaic Kingdom.

LUXOR TEMPLE

The Luxor Temple located on the east bank of the Nile River was dedicated to the god Amon. Many pharaohs participated in the construction of the temple and the final construction is a site to see as the night light illuminates the structures.

ALEXANDRIA

Alexandria was once a thriving city in Egypt as it was a major trading port and capital of Egypt. Alexander the Great was enamored with ancient Egyptian's knowledge of the arts and science and constructed a massive library from material all over Egypt. This library attracted people from all over the region.

TEMPLE OF PHILAE

The Temple of Isis was built to honor the goddess Isis and is located on the island of Philae, Egypt. Because of the frequent flooding on the island, the temple was relocated to the island Agilka.

EGYPT'S
LOCAL COMMUNITY

Egypt is currently a blend of many cultures and as you travel throughout the country, you will see the influence of indigenous Africans, Asians, Greeks, Romans, Arabs and the British.

THE GREAT TEMPLES OF RAMESSES II AT ABU SIMBEL

In Upper Egypt, near the border of Sudan, there are two massive rock temples. Pharaoh Ramesses II took great lengths to express the love that he had for his beautiful wife, Queen Nefertari and had a temple carved out of the side of a mountain in 1260 B.C.E. These temples were built during the sixty-six year reign, the larger temple was dedicated to himself, and the second temple was dedicated to his wife, Queen Nefertari.

Through my extensive photographic quest examining more than five thousand images of ancient Egypt, I tried to represent historical findings that rightly attribute Egypt's true history and contributions to the world. The photographs attempt to expose a rich volume of history not necessarily reflected in many history books. I trust that I have produced a fresh photographic documentary of what still stands in Egypt today as it did more than four thousand years ago. I hope this book inspires readers to explore while stimulating an insatiable desire to study the true history of Africa.

"A people without the knowledge of their past history, origin,
and culture is like a tree without roots."
—*Marcus Garvey*

ACKNOWLEDGMENTS

I would be remiss if I did not mention the people who supported and inspired me to publish *African Legacy Uplifted: Ancient Egypt, Volume One*. I want to acknowledge Jerry Clarke, a lifelong educator and friend who changed the lives of many students. I also want to recognize Ashanti West, who instilled the importance of seeking out true history. I want to express my gratitude to Donna Thompson for her work encouraging students to step out on faith to achieve their dreams. And finally, I want to thank Dr. Reverend Oliver Davis, a lifelong mentor, for his encouragement and direction.

I want to thank my family, especially my daughters Gianna, Jocelyn, and Jasmine for their tenacious approach in striving to become their best self. I also want to show gratitude to my parents, Elizabeth Galloway McArthur and Raymond McArthur, Sr.; brothers and sisters Eleanor, Umar, Jenny, the late Arlene, Raymond, William, Debra, and Bernice; and the extended family, all of whom have inspired me throughout my life.

Sometimes friends are like immediate family members, and I want to thank Robert Thomas, Nathanial Amritt, Dora Salmon, Tony Lockhart, Timmy Williams, Luster Privitt, Arhea Clark, Cynthia Snipes, Dawn Sneed, Renee Wright-Parker, Lorenzo Marshall, and Vanessa Sansbury, for their unwavering support.

I also want to sincerely thank a host of family members and friends who have been with me every step of the way. There are too many of you to name, but I appreciate your significant impact on my life.

Made in United States
North Haven, CT
26 October 2023